HOUSE ᴏꜰ TONGUES

Susan Wicks has published three books of poetry with Bloodaxe Books: *House of Tongues* (2011), *De-iced* (2007), and *Night Toad: New & Selected Poems* (2003), which included a new collection with selections from three earlier books published by Faber: *Singing Underwater*, winner of the Aldeburgh Poetry Festival Prize; *Open Diagnosis*, which was one of the Poetry Society's New Generation Poets titles; and *The Clever Daughter*, a Poetry Book Society Choice which was shortlisted for both T.S. Eliot and Forward Prizes. Both *House of Tongues* and *Night Toad* are Poetry Book Society Recommendations.

She has published two novels, *The Key* (Faber, 1997) and *Little Thing* (Faber, 1998), a short memoir, *Driving My Father* (Faber, 1995), and a collection of short fiction, *Roll Up for the Arabian Derby* (Bluechrome, 2008). Her translation of Valérie Rouzeau's *Cold Spring in Winter* (Arc, 2009) won the Scott-Moncrieff Prize for French Translation, and was shortlisted for both the International Griffin Poetry Prize and the Oxford-Weidenfeld Prize.

Born and raised in Kent, she lives in Tunbridge Wells.

SUSAN WICKS

HOUSE OF TONGUES

BLOODAXE BOOKS

First published 2011 by
Bloodaxe Books Ltd,
Highgreen,
Tarset,
Northumberland NE48 1RP.

www.bloodaxebooks.com
For further information about Bloodaxe titles
please visit our website or write to
the above address for a catalogue.

Supported by
**ARTS COUNCIL
ENGLAND**

Cover design: Neil Astley & Pamela Robertson-Pearce.

Printed in Great Britain by
Bell & Bain Limited, Glasgow, Scotland.

CONTENTS

ACKNOWLEDGEMENTS

Acknowledgements are due to the editors of the following publications in which some of these poems have already appeared: *Agenda*, *Alhambra Poetry Calendar*, ed. Shafiq Naz (Alhambra Publishing, 2008, 2009 & 2011), *Blackbox Manifold*, *Contourlines: New Responses to Landscape in Word and Image*, ed. Neil Wenborn and M.E.J. Hughes (Salt Publishing, 2009), *Did I Tell You? 131 Poems for Children in Need*, ed. Nicky Gould & Vicky Wilson (Categorical Books, 2010), *The London Review of Books*, *Magma*, *The New Orleans Review*, *Of Love and Hope*, ed. Deborah Gaye (Avalanche Books, 2010), *Poetry London*, *Poetry Review*, *The Rialto*, *Smith's Knoll*, and *Women's Work: Modern Women Poets Writing in English*, ed. Eva Salzman & Amy Wack (Seren, 2008).

'The Cricket Pitch Bells' was written as part of a shared writing/visual art project called *Re:Collections* inspired by the hidden collections of Tunbridge Wells Museum, for exhibition in the town's Art Gallery in January/February 2011.

Unattributed quotations in the *Nightwatchman's Yard* sequence are from Britt Svensson's *Guide to Visby* (Gotlands Fornsal, 2001).

I am particularly grateful to The Baltic Centre for Writers and Translators in Visby, Sweden, the MacDowell Colony, and the Virginia Center for the Creative Arts in Virginia and Auvillar, Tarn et Garonne, where I worked on many of these poems.

Pistachios

A darkening January afternoon.
I stand at the kitchen window absently eating
pistachios left over from Christmas; outside, a blur
of hydrangea as I slide
the edge of my nail between the curved wings of a shell.
They say sex is a kind of dying.

At a certain time of life –
you never know exactly when
or where or how fast – sex leaves.
It's like a tide
slowly leaving a beach, imperceptibly exposing
rocks like bony fingers, hidden tongues of sand
and sometimes the rank on improbable rank
of mussels close as bristles –
millions of them, blue-black,
crowding the surface – like the teeth of combs
or petrified fur
that teases the soles of your bare feet
raw – a whole glittering expanse
of blue-black points, and, hidden inside,
that throb of flesh. As the tide recedes
a million brittle mouths lean shut.

A skeleton hydrangea bowls across the dusk,
shivers. I crack another shell open,
feeling saliva spurt
at the green thought
of pistachios, salt on my lips, shells light as paper.

French Kissing in Brittany

The days were endless, all those blue-grey fields
of artichokes stretching to the horizon
as I pedalled past
on a borrowed bike, my skin
a welt of hives. The nights sleepless,
white as ashes while the two French girls
checked out the clubs, crashing back in at four a.m.
to warm their sheets with whispered anecdotes.

Out there in the dark
the blockhouse hunched its concrete into rock.
One night I lay, the small round fists of stones
knuckling my spine, the sand
still sticky from the tide, and at my feet
a glitter like sea-glass. Well after midnight
and his mouth a cave
as I grope for the entrance,
meteors falling at the corners of my eyes.

Bracken

In the crack between rocks a man is
unzipping his fly. The tarnished teeth gape open
in a sagging zigzag. In his hand a purple flower,
an extra purple thumb, a hooded flower,
and he is stripping it of its goodness
till it pulses and the milky sap spills over
and the stem collapses, all its secret growing
filaments gone soft, the thumb broken.

I am glad the child I was crept out
along the sandy slit where the rock was broken
and fronds of bracken opened their tight fingers,
to find him waiting with his elsewhere face
and see his big hand moving, see the purple
hooded orchid pulse between his fingers.

Gods

They're lying together naked on a beach
somewhere in the Caribbean: clumps of palm
frame them in knife-blades as he leans
on one elbow to touch her, his sunlit arm
a swelling bed of flesh, his taut
skin modelled by sunlight. And she's laid out
before him, her Bardot face
pixelled in shades of brown. Her sunlit breast
hangs like a mango, ripe enough to pick, as if
painted by numbers. Just that suggestive twist
of something not quite human
somewhere in the region of her waist.

Here, among chickens and olives, shellfish, toasters,
piled-up apricots and peaches,
bolts of cotton cloth, and espadrilles and purses
someone is going to buy this
image on canvas; someone will choose wool
in all the required colours, to cover them thread by thread;
pierce their reclining bodies over and over
with a big-eyed needle under the TV's flicker,
a radiator gurgling at her elbow,
or in summer, drowned in the apple tree's green shadow

till they rise together, mounted on card
and framed in mock mahogany, to hang over the bed
where she'll lie beside him waiting
for bats, for sleep, for the echoes of feet and voices
to fade downhill,
for dawn,
for the church clock
to shudder the walls awake –
while the fan moves its slow head from side to side.

Red Squirrel

He is a paradox, each tiny stitch
is running motionless. Towards the tree
he leaps, he's about to streak up,
he never reaches it
completely. Each patient cross
doubles back on itself.

Nothing about him is continuous,
nothing relaxes, tenses.
Yet he runs,
his muscles bunch, our mind
supplies the rest. An hour in bad light
beside a tree that sprouted

twig by twig, she squinted by her window,
held up her needle,
sharpened the wet thread
on her tongue, and he hung invisible
as an unborn thought.

He is frozen,
racing. Look how he sits
on his haunches, all quick-praying paws
and ears and careful eye-glint,
as an unseen wind
travels his fur – then bounds away,

his tail like a signature, leaving his ghost
to fray in the canvas.

La Fileuse
Jumilhac-le-Grand

She's lived in this chamber of blood
for thirty years, a bee in a sweet cell,
vines writhing across the walls
at the tip of her paintbrush, pulsing their deep red
trumpets towards the ceiling, swelling in clots of fruit.

This letter-slot was her mouth: this geometric hole
where they'd pass in the steaming food.
Sometimes they'd hear her humming at the wheel,
tapping her rhythmic foot,
and picture the coils of thread
that spilled from her fingers in a gleaming pile.

What kept her here by herself
was nothing as explicable as death
of love: her vines have tracked and tentacled the walls
till she has nothing but her own skin
to paint on, hardly a finger-space to breathe.

These are her last needs
concealed in a tangled skein
thrown from the casement: an empty dish;
brushes of squirrel-hair or sable; spirit burner; dyes;
a needle sharp enough to prick the patterns in.

The Cricket Pitch Bells

The fifteen bells were worn by the horse team driven annually by the Steward of the Manor of Rusthall across the cricket pitch on the Common to assert the rights of the freeholders.

How quietly they wait
down here in the dark –
fifteen of them, sisters –
strung to their own oak,

dangling motionless,
some of them untuned
to a metallic round
they never learned.

Just once a year
he'd reach to lift them up
stilling them with his fingers,
undo the straps

and free them, one after another,
discover them like treasure
under the scalloped canopy's
cracked leather.

What could their bodies tell
cupped in his palm?
Did they ring cold and hollow
under his thumb?

Did he bend and breathe
his breathy cloud,
rub their skin yellow
on the turn-up of his sleeve?

They hardly cared
how they felt or looked
on a team of skewbalds, just
that today they were spared

and twelve months of silence
burst from their gullets,
sharpened his argument
like so many bullets.

Then here they'd hang
strapped to this rigid thing,
their metal dulled,
their bodies shivering

to think how in a shriek
they'd opened their brass mouths
and let their iron tongues
bang back and forth;

how the message jangled
out across the land
like a warning, ringing
all he stewarded with sound.

No danger the men in white
might quietly make off
with a chain of sunlit turf
that was his by right.

At his horses' necks
they rang out, *Mine! Mine!*,
heavy as metal bollocks.
They were his last, best tune.

Now they're all locked up
in darkness. They wait
far from the grass,
the shadows inching out

from every stone and stick,
the lost ball snagged
in branches, the munching beasts,
the Sunday cricketers.

Crow

An easy mistake to make
for both of you – to fly through air
and find yourselves trapped here
among rafters, knocking your wings
on the low-slung metal bells
of ceiling-lights that clang
when you hit them, into a hard sky
you find you can't fly through,
the two of you swooping so close
that either of you could have been leader
by a feather. But somehow your mate
has found her own way out
into sunlight, where the insects
rise and fall in a lit cloud.
You let yourself drop
under the open window, your heart
a flicker of beating blood
through feathers. Then you hop up
to the sill and, look, suddenly you're back
in the world of the flying –
just a splatter of elderberry crap
on my lino, your fear a dark star.

Nuclear

Each morning as I round the bend,
the same shock –
                  that flash of river light, the bridge,
the cooling-towers –
                  always that first sight gasp
as if they've been dropped there –

Yet the landscape knows them: a fragment of old stone
moves sideways, and through a tangle of red
the river glitters, the bridge
spins out its turquoise cobweb and there they stand
like a cruet – squat on the flood-plain, lit
apricot, steaming quietly into this end of night.

I've heard there's a place where fish
swim up and down a ladder, mouthing through murk
like cruising angels;
                  where a student strung himself up for days
from a concrete cliff while the canal
sent back his image;
                  where they hand out packages of pills
to every household, in case of leaks.

But here at my open window the field's
rippled with leaves, and blue,
                  the every morning noise
of cockcrow, unidentified shadows finger-flapping across.

Cycling to See the Fish-ladder

Do they riffle their translucent fins
between the rungs to inch up?
Or do they effortlessly rise
as if through someone's sleep
to do what people do
with ladders – search and replace
a frost-cracked tile, or shake a tree
into a waiting skirt? Each trunk I pedal past
swells and shrills with cicadas before it fades.

But when, blinded by sweat, I finally arrive
the ladder's shut
by a Red Alert. *Merci
de votre compréhension.* I straddle my bike
and read what power means
to fish and spawning-grounds. I think I understand:
a glitch and the dream floats belly-up,
the waters of the Garonne
log-jammed and stinking. There's only the sky's

unbroken blue, the tree's small pool of shadow,
a woman's leaning bike. Nothing you can pull out
in a shining shaft, no wooden feet
to dent the mud,
no uprights you can steady against death.

WHAT SHE WAS

Deer in Summer

(for Bridget)

She came as we walked one evening
in a field of blond corn: just a ripple of barley
in low sunlight, and her back
appearing above it in a sudden arc
like a brown dolphin, accompanying us nearly
to our door, as dolphins sometimes accompany a ship.

That night, the storm. Before it broke,
the sound of something snuffling in our kitchen,
tearing at plastic with its claws and teeth
in a trail of yoghurt-pots. Then the lightning came closer,
closer, against the black
as the nut tree at the window
started to thrash its snapping limbs and shriek

and I seemed to see her leaping
through the standing barley to a dry place
with her unseen fawn. Now as the fine hairs rise
on our arms, while I shiver
imagining the breaking of the next wave,
I want to believe
they lie together nestled in a deep
hollow lined with leaves, and sleep out the thunder.

Cover

All morning the tractors have been trundling across
our field, outlined against sky
or down there in the valley, muffled, then turning up
behind us with another swathe of cut hay
when we see the deer again,
a brownish streak between seedheads – caught
in her panic to escape
the dust, the metallic thunder,
while a tide of flattened grass laps at the green
trapezium she stands in, in a rout
of fieldmice and crickets, frogs, grasshoppers and larks
shrilling their fear between the last stalks.

Where were we when the frantic creatures broke
and flew for cover? We must have been out
paddling our fibreglass canoe
through the shallows, learning to shift our weight
into deeper water; or was it later
as we strolled the alleyways and galleries of stone
in search of that carved Last Judgement, its faceless shape
sinking in an abraded pan –
or was it a leaky boat?

When she makes her final leap across the sunlit stubble
every last thought is gone.

Deer Grazing

She barely looks up from her grass
at the sound of feet, filling her soft skin
before winter, but as I run past
her deep eyes seem to hold everything
in stillness. If I were up close

I'd see myself red-faced
in my kit and trainers, pausing to let my heart
subside in my throat and the day
tick gently, a plane drifting across.

That world in her eye
could crumble, burst into flame,
and the tiny people float down
like ash, their final messages
make rings in her iris as they fly apart.

Deer in Darkness

I sensed rather than saw them move
in the darkness, the dark fractionally displaced
at the edge of seeing, and flowing back
invisible, the touch of a blind ghost –
identical molecules of air replacing one another
or a kaleidoscope where every piece
is black, and slides silently into place.
Just a flicker as something shied past –
starlight or winking plane, the gleam of silver
birch trunks swaying, fall of a frosted leaf –
was a tail waltzing alone on the dark grass
and something invisible had changed places,
stirred in the darkness, shifted, or stepped over.

Morning

First light. A whole small herd of deer
stands nudging at my glass door
with their noses, jostling one another,
their breath painting the pane silver,
each in her small slick of clear.

I open a crack
and in they streak
between door-jamb and frame
in a reek of matted hair and something trodden,
leaving their warm roughness on my hands.

The deer I know by day
are shy, wary of humans,
ready to leap into a dark place
with a flash of scut, but these

flow in and in like strands
of braided water, weaving and interweaving
till I have to wake
and feel their noses on my face,
my breasts, nudging between my thighs.

What She Was

She jumps silently away
through moonlight, startled, and at first
she's not herself: she's a rocking-horse
swaying on rockers buried deep under snow,
her tail a white paintbrush –
or she's some kind of small boat
making for harbour, plunging from crest to crest,
powder bursting all round her like spray.

Then she is what she is. As we drive away
I imagine her curled somewhere – just a deer in fresh snow,
forced to jump clear of a drift
into the trees' shelter. The moonlight sifting
between trunks was incidental. She was in too deep,
floundering, almost ungainly –
though there was grace there too: a slow V
widens behind her like a ship's wake.

And now I've lost her entirely.
Against a backdrop of sirens, streets, suburban houses,
she's no longer deer. She's barely
a silver rocking in the corner of my eye,
escaping towards woods. Yet something in me still pauses,
watches as she crests the wave and plunges,
feels itself blinded as she rises.

* * *

Le Vieux Lyon
(i.m. S.B.)

Do you remember Lyon, the old town
with its labyrinth of streets
and Lori's 'knit-shop' where she'd ask advice
about shaping, stitches? Remember that narrow light
from before, when walls almost touched
across alleys, and people could join hands?

How Scott bent his head and breathed
with his foot on the footrest, only the guitar
alert, and alternative lives
flitted across his features as he played;
how the knit-shop woman brought out her metre tape
for the raglan shoulder, scribbled something on paper –
slip one, purl one, pass the slipped stitch over –
mohair angora lambswool intertwined
in a ripple of slate and jade?

Remember that loose blue-grey
thing Lori once made you, with the enormous sleeves
where you'd hide dice or beads
from the children, then magic them back? He played
Scarlatti with that Frenchman, breathing himself asleep
to the music, while in the street outside
it got dusk, and swallows dived
to their nests, twittering under the eaves.

Sorry

(for Elkie)

The sky itself is simple,
its winter end of afternoon
bleeding imperceptibly from slate to green.
Only the branches of the tree
cut it into thousands of lit pieces
shivering with the force of the wind.

This morning while your mother still breathed
you sat at her bedside, saying
Sorry, sorry, sorry, whether or not she could hear,
your words air
from a world that was already far away
and complicated, forking and forking with each new branch.

Now her body is already
simplifying itself.
Everything you both said, everything you were together
is thrashing, many-fingered, rain-drenched
as trees on the horizon.

Untitled (wheelchair)

(Mona Hatoum, stainless steel and rubber, 97 x 50 x 84 cm)

I am the paralysed and the pusher, I am the air
circulating in the steel chair.

I am the wasted hand that lies
inert on the arm-rest, and the hand that cries

a line of blood-drops each time it goes to grasp,
slashed across the heart-line. I am that gasp

and the unseen body humped on the steel seat,
my side-by-side feet

aligned on the foot-rest, as the grey road rolls under.
I am the hunger

of crowds that come and stand beside, around, above
the wings of my naked blades – of love.

She has lost her voice

and will not get it back: it wandered out
into the street and kept on walking
where she couldn't call it. It walked out
through cat-tails and breathing marshes
to the lake, its feet hardly denting the water,
not thinking of thirst or hunger,
or worrying who might follow.

It walked over the fields singing
with its name on a hand-written label
so it could reach its destination.
It walked away from the war
still raging in her thin body,
travelling barefoot and hatless
to a place that might still be peaceful.

It travelled through low sun
and leaf-storms and early morning,
over ruts and frozen grasses
that spiked its soles with burning.
No luggage, no rusting handcart
piled with pots, no moth-eaten blanket,
no furniture it had no use for.

It didn't care who heard
its farewell to fear or yearning.
It simply walked away
out of earshot, with its naked head
held high, as far as it was able.

(i.m. J.S.)

Enough

(for animator Karen Aqua)

> *Animation: The action of imparting life, vitality, or motion;*
> *quickening; inspiration with courage; the technique by means of*
> *which movement is given, on film, to a series of drawings. (OED)*

This is your patient magic: time
slicing each second to a fan of frames
where nothing seems to move, and yet
coyote swells to fish and fish to bird
in a turning circle, and something flaps away.

Watch how this innocent bud
stretches and flowers in a pregnant cloud
of nuclear fallout; watch how the carved gods
shiver, how they leap frantic from the rocks.

You have captured time's shimmer,
the dance of erratic cells
vibrating inside the body like bright beads
stripped from the thread. A three-second sequence
takes you whole days.

I see you on your knees
with a pack of childhood crayons, as you try to catch
corpuscles inching forwards. How much
time do you have? How much
do I, does anyone? *Enough*

to ease these shaded bodies imperceptibly apart
and film them frame by frame,
while the world turns white and logs crumble to ash

then see them dance onscreen in a bright rush.

The Canterbury Mimes

What were they up to, silhouetted high
over the old city with its bristle of spires?
One braced his arm
over and over for a ball that never came
and belted it away; one smashed her racquet against sky
for a shuttlecock no one could see;
while a third stood casually twirling a loop of rope
over a stampeding herd
only she could follow. But something was there unseen
on the path, its neck
a weal risen under the rope,
the invisible shuttle trapped
between the meshes of no-net,
the ball caught
like a lobster in a cage of hope.

And something skittered down the green hill,
bouncing from roof to roof, and fell
to the gutter like a bird
and hopped away. Walking towards them along the path
I feinted, ducked
as I saw it coming. What was I thinking of?

But they were crazy and young,
why not? And it was nearly spring.

After the Exam-board Meeting

All morning, in low voices,
numbers have blurred and merged –
someone's future *condoned*
or *compensated*, labelled second class
by preponderance, by the invocation
of a lost clause. I stretch my aching arms,
wiggle my toes under the table
to unclog the veins.

Then I'm driving away
and there's something at the corner of my eye –
thistledown? insects? When I accelerate
I lose them briefly – then see them delicately alight
between the leaves of hedges,
caress an iron spike

while in the car ahead
a girl in a yellow dress
holds up her hand
and a stream of bubbles bobs across my bonnet,
bursts in perfect circles
on my windscreen. She's waving goodbye
in rings of emptiness.

Come back.
Come back and hold up your wand
to the passing air.
You created them out of nothing –
nothing but your own stillness
and the momentum of the car.

Horizontal

(for Suzanne Opton)

Was it death-in-life
or life-in-death, those photos you showed
of soldiers, resting their young heads
on a table? No trace of blood
or bruising, no gouged exit
from jawline to temple. No shrapnel
fused deep into the bone.
They were just ordinary men
who happened to be soldiers, in their twenties
and thirties, their skin, the whites of their eyes
unclouded. Only they were lying on their sides.

I've sat in this room too long
peering out between the slats of blinds
to where the willow weeps almost to the ground.
In front of my window
the shrubs have grown up and flowered
and been cut back, a new commemorative seat's
been set in place and people sit on it
to draw on cigarettes. Now rain
darkens the 60s buildings; somewhere a phone's ringing;
there's a sudden gust of music from the next room.

I rest my head
on the desk and let this sun-through-blinds
cut me to slivers. No blood,
no swollen lip, no bruising – just a woman's still face
on a pile of papers,
perhaps asleep.

Bypass

My first few years, it was a clean curve,
cars trickling down the cheek of the hill
between fields – and in the springtime, a ripple
of cowslips, pools of sunlight along the verge –
the traffic sliding downwards through green
into mist and glowing brake-lights
past turf that had lain years undisturbed.

Then steamrollers lumbered up and down
along a scar, through months of contraflow
in a mess of cones, splashes of spilt light
from dishes mounted above my head like guards
alert for movement – that jolt of surprise
at a ramp; a brake; a turn; a sudden chicane
or traffic-signal – till I came to the place
where smoke from the cement-works crawls up into sky.

One night driving back half-asleep
and dreaming of what I'd give
to leave it all, I must have followed a new sign –
and found myself somewhere I'd never been
between hillsides of saplings planted in geometric rows
like a shadow-graveyard. Out on that orbital road
from nowhere to nowhere I'm doing 50,
60, more, and no one alive

sees me disappear
through a bridge that wasn't there, no one sees me emerge
into nothing – just the blink of a cruising plane
in the glass of my windscreen, a few faint stars.

Virtual

(for Bridget)

This quest seems always the same:
a clash of weapons, flying grains of sand.
Only the backdrop changes
leaving you on a ledge, lost,
the drop vertiginous.
Is this what being young means,
this landscape of chasm and cliff,
where your life's a thin blue line,
renewable, and whatever it is you need
is hidden, always just out of range?

Just days ago you crossed the Pyrenees
in fog, trudging another slow mile
with nothing but the way itself.
No enemies, no rush of falling blades, no birds
swooping from overhead
in a scatter of black feathers. Only fatigue
and blisters, the path winding through low cloud
and a picnic of bread and cheese,

a goat out there somewhere, bleating.

Above Moissac, June

Sometimes our feet
would take us through orchards where the youngest trees
were heavy-red with cherries
left for the birds; sometimes along the verge
of neat allotments – beans and artichokes
like thistles, a hedge that breathed
boxwood, wild honeysuckle, roses.

Not even thought but only emptiness,
rustlings in undergrowth,
wild orchids poking up beside the path.
A field of sunflowers all turn their heads
as a deer leaps through.

Once, along a ridge towards late afternoon,
a line of drying clothes in every imaginable shade
of pink from early sunrise sugar mouse
magenta to ripe grape, maroon
and burgundy, the lees, the ring inside the glass.

The English Couples

Is it the quality of light
leaking from the walls of buildings
like an unkept secret, or the weeping planes
trailing their thin gold
in the water, swans drifting together and apart
between the leaves that float
like lace on the still surface? The bells
cough out their quarter-hours
over gilded scrollwork; fur
fringes the mouths of bridges.
A sudden smell of drains
gusts on a corner, as if a door
had swung suddenly open downstairs.

High over northern Europe, I saw the town
slide like a coin under my dark wing
and remembered stars
shaking in water: now I'm the one that blinks
and slips sideways as a street blurs
to a scallop of stepped gables
where the gentle English couples
walk up and down.

Fire-house

This is fire's official address –
a black façade, a Dutch interior
that frames a small domestic drama
inside a smoke-stained filigree of brass.
My fireplace is Flemish: its sturdy breast
a stepped gable, the covered flue-hole
a clock wiped of hours and minutes.

Inside are the vanished women,
their studious, leaning faces,
the fruit gleaming on a cloth, the fishes,
the lace and mahogany and jewels.
But the windows are all black-painted
and light is a square hole in the ceiling.
This is the fire-house to my canal

of painted floorboards, where I float past
on my barge of damask bedspread.
Here's where the crackle dies
between flame and flame, where a sluggish
smoke-breath beards the walls with soot
and the roofs of a collapsing city
whisper, worms flaring against brick.

House of Tongues

(after Paul Bowles' 'A Distant Episode')

We live in a house of tongues.
On the kitchen shelf
the clapper of the small brass bell
is shadow-hung.

Next to the back door
the tongues of our battered trainers
strain under laces, swell
crusted and luminous.

Across the back of a chair
your tie-collection slithers,
silky, alive between my fingers,
and tastes the air.

In this speaking place
I move carefully
from one room to another,
learning to defend myself.

If there were stones
I could stop and stoop
to pick them up,
filling my pockets.

At sundown the Reguibat come
to cut out the professor's tongue
and cover him with belts and necklaces
of tin, and set him clattering.

Screened Porch, December

On this old Adirondack chair,
my coat zipped right to the chin,
I'm a patient in a sanatorium.

My fellow-inmates are all dead,
their quaint belief in breath
long lost. The air is thinner here,

the cold pure ether of this place
fills my lungs as if from a great height:
I'm dying of some obsolete disease.

The sheep who grazed here once
are a vanished species. Twice
fire shrivelled the undergrowth.

Now the mountain's cone of ice
glitters through the receding trees.
Each day I breathe better.

Here on my blackened chair
while sun tickles the topmost firs
red-gold, I outlive myself.

Only a few obstinate leaves
still cling and rattle on the branches,
pattern my lap with their cold stars.

For Salt

(After Ulrike Koch's film, Die Saltzmänner von Tibet*)*

Here, where the air is thin
they cultivate slowness,
speak out of sun-blackened faces,
wrap their heads in hair like a black river.
Slowly they sever the thin carcass of a sheep
and lay it down, tighten the roped bundles,
follow the shaggy flock
of horns and swaying backs
dusted with white, to where the lake
mirrors the mountains like the flanks of beasts.

Here they pitch their tents,
and set themselves to labour, heaping the slow salt
in little hills like hives of whitish honey,
here where the wet salt weeps.
With the flat of a spade
they stroke them, heaping the crust dry
till the lake's pimpled all over
with lined-up salt-pots, gleaming between clouds.
They stroke and see the salt slide back
and heap it up again, filling the woven bags
almost too full to carry, stitch across the mouths.

Then even the yaks lumber
like old men in slippers, bearing the packed salt
on unsteady legs; their ankles waver
as if through heat-haze to the wind's shudder
here at the earth's cold heart. And soon
the caravan of men and animals is gone.

Now crusted trucks
crumble the crop between them and drive on
while back at camp among the toddling children
the storyteller stops her singing with a kind of sob,
the song itself over
and nothing to fill it, nowhere so high and far
and salty, nothing so crystalline again.

Under the Blue Umbrella

Under this blue inverted bowl
I live out summer
such as it is, while at the back of the sky
a kind of sun travels hazily from left to right
and I give my body up
to something resembling shade.

From a distant garden comes the monotonous
noise of what must be music: what carries
is only a single note
and a drum's repeated beat
under what could be voices: if I were closer
there'd be something human. Here on my blue planet
no one wails out his loss.

No one's heart clenches here. No one is seen to bleed
from the anus, or stand naked at a wall to be shot.
No one lies delirious at night
without a bottle. No one's strapped to a plank and immersed
till he forgets who he is.

The blue wheel seems to turn,
shifting with the movement of the sun,
creaking as it offers a sort of shelter
just for a few weeks
while we get out the plastic chairs, plant the lobelia.

Hickory Dickory

You were sleeping in my fleece's soft shade
and I shook you out
in a rain of gravel, like something dead.
Was it my body's heat

you were after, was it my dark,
my smell of human? Now it's too late.
Were you a mouse
or shrew? I'll never know.

The swallows skim the grass
for insects. Down in the river-bed
a mechanical saw's
a wailing wheel of splinters; a dog barks,
frantic, scrabbling at the wire with its paws.

I threw you out
of my sleeve
of waiting shadow, and you scurried off.

Sip

It sleeps under my tall glass
like a miniature princess
in a dark jersey – till I reach and undo the catch
and slide it out into the spring air
buzzing with sunlight. But it's a broken twig,
a clot of rotting leaf,
the way it plummets to the gravel path
and lies there, wings shivering.

Next time I'll lift one gently on card
to a sun-warmed ledge and wait
for the air to ruffle its fur;
inch by quarter-inch I'll watch it persevere
towards a patch of moisture
and sip, with something like a tongue.

Not drink, not guzzle. Only a few first drops
sticky with airborne pollen. Not
like a captive on the march
who'd fall on a gleaming cache
of jams, sausages looping from a high hook
above his head, a cellar stacked with roots,
and die there, racked with cramps.

Below us, clover, wild orchids, buttercups.
I see it slowly, slowly open its stuck wings
and waver, shuddering itself strong.

Into Silence

(after Philip Gröning's film, Le Grand Silence*)*

Afterwards I think how quietly he made
his brothers' habits, laying the fabric flat on a board
and pulling the selvedge straight, working quietly
in winter light with measuring tape and scissors,
moving unhurriedly from side to side
and folding, unrolling a bolt of cloth
and silently taking what he needed,
silently putting each unnecessary thing away.

How would it be to spend a life
endlessly pinning and tacking in a quiet room
as the sun moved slowly from one window to another
and shadows lengthened across the table,
to sew the long straight seam under the arms
and down each side, and along the centre of the hood,
hemming the heavy skirts by hand, the all-concealing sleeves?

It would be better without faith,
the room truly only a bare room
and nothing in it but cloth
and table, sunlight, scissors, pins and tape,
the steady slanting of time
as you sagged and stiffened, your body disgraced by age
like his, so that all the spaces that might have held belief

were open, empty, available,
echoing with height and winter,
the need to go on working quietly,
the need to love, to take care of the body.

Black Dog

Sometimes it would almost be enough
to have back just those few yards of path
I could see from my window,
frozen tyre-tracks curving
into the fir trees, slither of gritted hill
to the bend, where no one went down or up
but the truck or snowplough
and every weekday as I ate my lunch
a woman with a dog
leaping and bounding. After they'd passed
I'd find its flower-footprints
melting on gravel. Sometimes its breath
steamed, and sometimes dispersed unseen
like mine. Sometimes it stopped
to sniff or defecate, then it would make a run
to catch its other self, all sudden streak
of muscle, bunched under the warm fur.
I never heard it bark. She never
called. I never saw
her solid limbs break stride (the lead
swung loose between her fingers),
never even saw her searching with her eyes –
not sensing herself watched, not bothered
whether her astonishment of dog
ran on or lingered.

Inside the Movement

The sea spreads its blue fingers, light
white as a bandage, and seems to say, *Rest*,
and under the rest, movement,
inside the movement, sand
sinking softly, each grain glittering.

The gorse dies and dries back
to skeletons that are the opposite of dramatic,
replaced by a solid bank of yellow bloom,
the little pea-flowers crowded on each spiny stem
alive with bees, protecting themselves
and dying anyway, as others take up the shout.

Or birds. Or sheep. Or clumps of blowing wool
on barbs of wire. What does it matter?
The coastline itself is changing, a river silted over,
a lake dried up, a new sandbar created,
a section of cliff collapsing overnight

as if the land itself had had a stroke
and stared at us next morning lop-sided
with a drooping eyelid, its lobster-pots exposed.
We're built for loss. The sea goes out and out
leaving only plastic bottles, a single sandal,
a few chipped shells.

                    Then unaccountably comes in
right to the cliff-face, swirls its forgotten white.

Wings

Early morning through the bathroom window
the sound of pigeons, like the air itself –
the sound waiting inside a bell
before it starts swinging, or echoing back and forth
over the fields when the clapper's finally still.

They come round again, and the air's lung
fills and empties; the town wakes
and takes on colour, sun over slate and brick,
flashing in panes of glass.
The air gasps
each time they circle their loft.

One day they'll be crated up and shipped off and released
and I'll hear
not the same tight climb
of the fly-past, but that other beat
of wings across distance, pigeons returning home.

Girl with a Red Umbrella

It was a high red dome
of cloth, black-spotted, some kind of bug –
a ladybird –
             and she stood beneath it speechless,
pink in its reflected glow.

The two white crescents of its eyes
were two white flags on a billow of red sail

or pennants fluttering slowly down
through layers of grey air

to land her safely here at the glass door.

Is there any way to write about her?
Something I hardly know

clutches and opens,
                     starts to run warm
and I shut it off.

             But isn't it possible
to see a red umbrella over a tiny girl
and think of – what?
                     – the *oh*, the *ah*,
the *yes* of it, the laugh

that's something like hope?
             At her side her father
touches her small elbow
and smiles, seeing my face. He nudges her gently

gently forward, under the collapsing ribs.

Transparent

It was world and yet no world,
a monochrome still that slowly began to breathe,
the dapple water-lily floor
adrift in dry ice, and the white
skirts floating while the arms unbent
like breathing tendrils, as empty space
met decomposing space and the body breathed,
altered its shape as one.

Whoever in this place
had loved, whatever the protagonists' story,
whatever spells they cast –
there was only this breathing death
that could last for years,
this silvery moonlit place that hardly moved,
the bony backs
prostrated over the satin toes
and lightly breathing, the arcs of arms
like wings, like necks, neither bird nor human,
of those trapped swans
inhabited by girls
grieving for their lost selves.

And Siegfried and Odette, what did they know
with their either or,
their good or evil, black or white,
Odette or Odile? They were oblivious.
Out there the world
is silver, silver-grey, grey-white,
and swans lie breathing on a lake
in a dream of flight, and shimmer.

L'Après-midi d'un faune

(after Debussy and Mallarmé)

It's a study in half-sleep,
in moving branches seen through two slits,
a dapple of leaves

lengthening in sunlight, tendrils half in love
with empty air, of something swaying
unreachable above.

He listens: somewhere there's water
trickling, half-guessed –
and women laughing – or is it nakedness?

Everything is not yet –
is any moment – a sunlit space
beyond the weeping willow's travesty of loss.

Everything glistens, soon
to bead his flesh with sap, with milky blood
writing the tracks of thorns.

Box

The bush at my window holds the ghost of bird
and feathers it with leaves. Some topiary intent
coaxed it alive, and left. I can just make out
the flick of a frozen tail, a pecking head,

the mounds of folded wings, a form that blurs
with each small coming leaf. Daily it grows
away from gravity, towards the light,
daily becomes less bird, and more completely bush.

I see it and then I don't – how the greening spears
of box could open their wings and fly,
leave only a shorn-off stump.

The artist stands and stretches, glances at the sky,
the fields and woods, the distant purple hump
of the mountain, puts away his shears.

Cappella Catharinae in Visby Cathedral, September 2008

Even the deaf would hear
this music, its steady afternote
released years later, buzzing in the stone's throat.

Each vowel prolongs itself
in every pillar, each vibrating arch;
this place insists our voices are provisional.

However clear and crisp
we write our human music, this
discordant echo is the cathedral's voice.

The singing rises, builds
and shivers, hangs in a trapped chord
that stings our ear-drums, swelling behind the words.

Over

They swoop from all directions like birds
to land on this green cliff
above the cathedral. Their bicycles
lie propped in grass, the wheels ticking.

What is it they've come to watch?
Is it something holy? Their capes are bells
swelling in silence. They've come together
to talk wordlessly among themselves.

Under a small awning
a woman stands, her long dress blowing,
her wimpled features framed as if by bandages.
Something is about to happen.

And what is she carrying, a precious gift?
Can this be the birth of someone?
But she is erect and pale and willowy
and the watchers hunch, pulling their hoods lower.

This must be some northern story
that calls for rain, a pewter sky,
the gold-tipped branches of a spreading tree.
I hear them murmur as they drift closer,

scooping their bikes from the wet grass
and scooting downhill, yelling to one another,
Hej då, hej! as the clouds part
on a gleam, and something seems to be over.

NIGHTWATCHMAN'S YARD

Confession

Visby, 1350

I was the one who did it, poisoning the wells,
the black standing water, crusting them with scum.
I dropped my hate like a small stone
and heard it hit bottom.
Each Sunday I played your rotten organ to the town
as the ranks of faces quavered, gaping in unison.
You were mostly old,
loosing your warbled notes
to twitter and wheeze and die as the sexton growled
and twitchy children whined to be let out.
Meanwhile the priest droned on
self-righteous, his eyes not straying once
to the widow's cleavage – though I almost felt
his rod under the surplice like a one-man tent.

And how I worked, pumping the same sour air
and trying to make it sing
a better music, alone. Each night she battered the south door
to kneel beside him, whispering her sins.
I practised more; ate little; slept
a couple of hours a night; drank ale
till a stranger seemed to stand between my eyes –
a Jew, you'd say, no doubt.
I walked with my Jewish friends
and pissed in your well-shafts, sicked up my stomach's slime
and crapped on the cobbles, smeared it inside the pail.

Now I can let my voice
howl in your pipework, echo to the town walls:
how I spit on each upright soul
in this stinking city. Sure as this egg
that swells in my armpit, black as its breath of pus,
this bruise like a map of Europe – raised as the scars
you'll know my body by

58

when you see it lifeless. Bright as the flames
leaping from the candle-corners of this room
and the faces in them
tutting, guiltless, smooth as ever: his and hers.

Little Ingeborg

Behold my hands thus rendered through tribulation;
so ill is my suffering that I felt so faint-hearted as to
confess to more than I know.

A woman alone
with her child and her childs child
has to be djävul-sent. They smiled
as they drog me down.

My hands already ailed,
the knogs cricked hard
as slang-shot birds. My gaolers had
a pretty thing for nails.

They set it on. I howled
till the walls gave back
and every finger bruck.
They blindad me and tied me to a stol

then dyked me in the wet,
one gång, ten gånger, hiked me aluft
till I heaved and spat
my teeth on strängs. They laughed.

Ja så. And I confessed
to whatsohelst they asked –
the sickdom, the hail and frost
to spoil their harvest.

They left me here
for years, where the råtskinns rot
by the iron grate
like so many stiff tears.

But I milk their koos
as I used to from my bed
with a par knivblad while they doze,
and the milk runs red.

St Drotten and St Lars

Both sisters hated each other to such an extent that they
couldn't even go to the same church. When their father died and
the sisters divided the estate, each sister built herself a church.

It wasn't exactly hate; it was something subtler
that laid our churches out: I overheard
her laughing on the stairs
with our father – intimate, as if his younger daughter
were more to him than that – and then he died.

Whatever she believed
was not enough; she'd take what cash she could
and build a church as big as she imagined
him dead in – corners not quite true
and the pillars striped, the ceiling decorated to distraction.

You wouldn't catch me there
with a lighted candle, down on my knees
in a fug of worship, under a pillar like a stick of rock,
those painted curlicues and ochre eagles' feathers
trailing, smeared across the plaster!

Mine grew stone by stone
among the scratching hens
and huddled cottages. I often visited.
I stood in the dust of limestone, looking up.
The masons knew me, high on their scaffolding.

I went for the simple cross,
the round Byzantine arch
like the ends of fingers, passages,
a flight of unexpected stairs – where a line of nuns
might file in darkness with fireworks in their hands
acting their Ruin Plays.

The Ruined Churches

They lie here, great shells of nothing
beached above the Baltic,
the ceilings long crumbled among weeds,
the glass and painted plaster
flaked back to bare stone.

Yet the arches reach; intrepid
tufts of yellowed fern
flutter from ledges; a flurry of bats or birds
quickens a wall with shadow, as if even the design
were ruin, intended emptiness,

and ruin joyful. Witness
a town's inexorable fall from grace
as merchant stronghold; witness this harbour
we walk on, this patch of sky
shining through masonry.

So much belief
paid for in wine and timber, leather, candles, sheep
and fancy goods, so many markets lost,
so many sacred doorways
padlocked, dangerous.

Aurora Sprit

At first it was nothing, a little weal
on the skin of my cheek
that grew bossy, complicated as a Viking shield
and reddened at the heart. Then one day as I ate
I dropped the ladle. When they teased and poked
I hardly felt them. Somehow I'd turned
to a lump of limestone fossil-printed with fern.

Now I live here at St Göran's with the rest:
the legless, lipless, melted, holes
for ears and noses. Outside the town walls
we make our bird-scare music. We may be shut out
but you hear our clapper voices, inside.

In a few hundred years
they'll have cured this sickness, the lazarett
razed to its foundations, the church barred,
the floor a welter
of seedlings, sycamore and elder. By the south door,
rolling half-hidden in the long grass
a broken bottle says *Aurora Sprit*. At daybreak
through mist I wander down
to the shoreline, watch the milky water swell
like breathing to the stone's cheek.

Galgberget

Back then you could see right across
from these three pointing fingers
leprous with lichen, past the cathedral spires
to the market-place
teeming with men and cattle. The warehouses,
their gables climbing to heaven step by step.
To seaward, ships
lying low at anchor, fishing-boats scattered
like birch twigs along the coast.
But they were blindfolded.

It was the townspeople who saw
these three stone stumps
and the ring of wall that held them
pressed against cloud.
The bodies like dark sacks
tied off at the necks.

They might have seen oarless ships
and giant birds; that the beams would rot
and children play here, balancing, arms outstretched;
that what they believed
would leave a dozen churches
roofless, untenanted.

But the ones who climbed
past a jeering crowd
of the customers they cheated,
what did they see reflected
in the dismissive eyes? The ends of churches
riddled with ivy? Themselves?

Dust

Lord Ivar of Visborg Castle sent Matts the Cobbler
as his proxy on a pilgrimage to Compostela.

It's not like making shoes. For years
I've stretched and dyed
and stitched, and sent them out
to the townsfolk, even across the Baltic –
my babies' bootees lined with curly fleece,
my calfskin slippers, my soles and uppers.
The day I left my master
standing on the quayside and took ship
they walked the gangplank with me in matching pairs
and followed me to Danzig, tramping by day-stages
to Berlin and on through Innsbruck, and into France.

Now I've grown to love
this landscape – cherries left spoiling on the young trees
for thieves or birds, a vineyard turning red
on a sun-striped hillside. Even this dust
that coats me, tanning my northern skin
to basan: I'm free to walk
wherever the path might lead. Though when I lie
a long white night among the bloody signatures
of bugs, I wake too early
and stumble on. No wonder my good master
cited his duties, preferring to stay home.

And Compostela? Well,
it isn't Visby. Not at all. The miracles I saw
were small and happened everywhere
along the road. And as for the stone boat
I never quite believed it hadn't sunk
after the stones and ships
I've seen at home in Gotland –
knowing them opposites.

But the oddest thing is shoes –
no longer to call myself cobbler
but only the one who wears
the *stövlar*, *Schuhe*, *chaussures*
in *fårskinn*, *cuir* or *cordován*,
whatever you like to call it. My hands have hardened,
stiff from the staff; even the old techiques
are subtler now – the *skomakarsapparat* –
the awls and trenkets, turnsticks, lasts
and hogshair needles new-fangled,
the nallies neater, iron black more black.

I ask you, how would my dear master
have proceeded? He would have been prevented,
laying down rations in his well-stocked cellars –
hams and drying herrings and old wine –
paying his garrison,
pacing the crowded quayside up and down.
Or raising his tankard, rolling his new mistress
in a knot of sheet, his toes and heels
still silky, innocent of blisters,
his soles upturned.

The Plundering of Visby

(after C.G. Hellqvists's painting, Valdemar Atterdag brandskattar Visby, *1882)*

Let them go forth and torment one another.
SELMA LAGERLÖF

The town belongs to me, its booths and barrels,
half-timbered buildings, roofs and marketplace,
its wailing women slumped like waiting sacks –
one slit and they run empty – these frantic folk
with their up-to-heaven eyes. Whereas
I'm no one. Before me the crowd parts
as if before a blade. Between their feet I stride
and leave an open wound, and the town's water
oozes red as rust, the sides of ships
signed with a rusty tidemark. Here in the casks
the treasure mounts, the coins and necklaces,
the plate. Let them eat off wood,
adorn themselves with seaweed, wait
for the metal to flow back; let them light fires
in the forges' outer circle, and begin again.

The horses stamp and whicker. Round the town
the merchants idle, waiting for new coin
in a swarm of flying sparks, their backs covered
with a gleam like flame. This place is mine
and I vacate it. Now my banked oars flash,
the ship slides out along the walled harbour
towards the open sea, and they fall on one another
scratching and biting, taking an eye out,
an ear, a tongue, a penis, so when I look back
and see the town reflected, cliff and gable,
steeples, warehouses and market
dyed with rust, I think how even streets
are paved with metal, how the metal bleeds.

Nightwatchman's Yard

I light my small fire under the arcades
and watch the shadows flicker in the yard.
No danger my eyes will close: the giant necks
and knees still play over the rocks,
the ropes that tied the hands, the blindfolds I tightened.
Till all they could see
was a crescent of daylight, the stars on their own cheeks.
And if that wasn't enough,
there's the sheep and goats, the horse-flesh fit to eat
and the rest, the ones that shiver,
too old and broken even to cry wolf,
their manes and fetlocks clotted, dagged with trash,
heads in the gutter, ribs like a church roof.
I watch the blood run free
between the cobbles, turning the moss
to sodden velvet. But at work one day,
as I scoured the hidden chamber of a latrine
in a rich man's house, the turds slithered away
and I saw a ruby glinting like a red eye.

Sometimes in the daytime when he thinks I'm asleep
I watch him go about
his dirty duties, and I feel clean. All I do is hear
their sorry mumbles, tie their shaking hands
and set them moving, cover their eyelids with cloth.
All I kill are beasts
who don't know what it is
to be human, never think to wait
for the axe to bite. The dirt
is someone else's. Yet the nights
are endless in this place. Only at midday
when the little tune plinks out from the cathedral
do I sometimes wake
from a dream of childhood, when I used to climb
the trees outside the walls, the blossom
falling through sunlight, heavier than smoke.

You can imagine what goes on
in that heaving shack, between the tarred excuse
for chimney and the chicken-feathers. You can see it rise
from the roof and it smells bad,
bad, the rain-puddles in the yard
rank with old blood and piss.

Sometimes you can hear noises,
the neighing of horses
or is it the sound she makes
when they have sex? She's barely visible –
just the barefoot kids with purple-mottled ankles,
a zigzag chicken squawking to escape a cart.

When she deigns to show her face
with a basket of dirty laundry, if you sneak a look
the clothes are all flea-specked,
wrinkled, stiffened with God knows what.
Later you see them sway
limbless through drizzle in the early morning.

And he's a stick, a dry one. Our nightwatchman!
What does he watch? He's off
with the smallfolk. Sometimes you catch the children
streaking in all directions like pale rats
and you know she's got him
ploughing the sucking darkness, while she laughs.

Sometimes I show him my body.
He's seen so many
faces indigo with blood,
the tongues pushed out
and swollen, crusted with salt and soot.

Sometimes I give him rope
and he ties my hands and feet,
fashions a scratchy noose
as the children scamper,
leaving their pale footprints in the grease.

When he's cut down a thief,
untied the blindfold,
seen the white eyes staring through the cloth,
I can almost smell it on him
like garlic. Sometimes he coughs

or labours, wears himself out
bumping and straining.
Then he holds me hard-pressed
against his heartbeat
till it finally shudders and goes quiet.

He'd be better gone.
By summer I'll throw him out
replace him with someone younger.
His thin-lipped master
paces, a few doors down.

A few months yet
and I'll have the new one pissed
and naked, only his hangman's hood –
feed him my nipples
through the blackened slit.

On summer evenings from their cottage on the north cliff
you can hear her clear voice singing through the dusk

at almost midnight, one of the thousands of new ghosts
that haunt this film-set. As the sea turns red

the gap between the Baltic and its bank of cloud
fills with unlikely flame. And then it's gone

and Kajsa's voice goes silent. Jacob did his best
to keep their lives afloat. When the sea was too angry

for little boats, he'd strip himself naked,
swim to the ship at anchor in the harbour,

the town's official letters clenched between his teeth,
like a dog with a newspaper. He was only

trying to teach his young successors how to swim
as well as he did, when a wave of Baltic sunset

swelled in the distance, flooded the waiting chamber of his brain.

The Doomsday Fish

Where did they hang it – here in the nave
in a pool of glassy light, or from one of the chandeliers
that dangle so low over the pale aisle
they almost brush our heads? Or from a window-ledge
high on the north side, to seaward
with a view of the swelling Baltic? Or from the pulpit
with its helter-skelter steps? But they came later.
The church was smaller then, empty of furniture.

At any rate it fell
not once, not twice,
not three times even, when the gates of Hell
were supposed to burst open: it flopped and flopped
in a slither of falling fish, and lay
like a shoe worn thin with walking,
till they threw it in an attic and left it to dry
to Peking duck, its prophesying life over.

Or perhaps they pinned it to a small cross
by its lateral fins, above the rough altar
where a pilgrim once saw it gasp
and arch its spine and writhe, and cry like a baby
hungry for love, as it had the day they found it
under the first foundations, in the spring's clear water.